www.raintreepublishers.co.uk
Visit our website to find out more information about Raintree books.

To order:
☎ Phone 0845 6044371
🖨 Fax +44 (0) 1865 312263
✉ Email myorders@raintreepublishers.co.uk

Customers from outside the UK please telephone +44 1865 312262

Raintree is an imprint of Capstone Global Library Limited, a company incorporated in England and Wales having its registered office at 7 Pilgrim Street, London, EC4V 6LB - Registered company number: 6695582

First published by Raintree in 2013
The moral rights of the proprietor have been asserted.

Originally published by DC Comics in the U.S. in single magazine form as Superman Adventures #1. Copyright © 2012 DC Comics. All Rights Reserved.

Ashley C. Andersen Zantop *Publisher*
Michael Dahl *Editorial Director*
Donald Lemke & Sean Tulien *Editors*
Heather Kindseth *Creative Director*
Bob Lentz *Designer*
Kathy McColley *Production Specialist*

DC COMICS
Mike McAvennie *Original U.S. Editor*
Bruce Timm *Cover Artist*

ISBN 978 1 406 25403 7
16 15 14 13 12
10 9 8 7 6 5 4 3 2 1
Printed and bound in China by Nordica.
0512/CA21200799
British Library Cataloguing in Publication Data
A full catalogue record for this book is available from the British Library.

SUPERMAN ADVENTURES

Men of Steel

Paul Dini............................... writer
Rick Burchett ....penciller
Terry Austin .... inker
Marie Severin .... colorist
Lois Buhalis....................... letterer

Superman created by
Jerry Siegel & Joe Shuster

MEN OF STEEL

Paul Dini - Writer
Rick Burchett - Penciller
Terry Austin - Inker
Marie Severin - Colorist
Lois Buhalis - Letterer
Mike McAvennie - Editor

SUPERMAN CREATED BY JERRY SIEGEL AND JOE SHUSTER

"In three years on the Planet's city desk, covering everything from gun running to garbage strikes...

"...this reporter had never seen anything like it."

SURE, HE *SEEMS* TO HAVE EVERYONE'S BEST INTERESTS AT HEART, BUT AS A REPORTER, I NEVER TAKE *ANYONE* AT FACE VALUE...

...ESPECIALLY IF THEY CAN FLY!

CAN'T BLAME YOU THERE. WHAT ABOUT YOU, RON? ANGELA?

I THINK IF SUPERMAN HAD AN ULTERIOR MOTIVE, WE'D HAVE SEEN IT BY NOW, CHIEF. HE'S ONLY BEEN IN TOWN A FEW DAYS AND ALREADY HE'S SAVED DOZENS OF LIVES.

THE GUY'S *DEFINITELY* FOR REAL.

YOU CAN SAY THAT AGAIN! SUPERMAN'S THE HOTTEST STORY TO HIT METROPOLIS IN YEARS!

I'M RUNNING EYEWITNESS ACCOUNTS IN MY COLUMN, PLUS EXCLUSIVE FOOTAGE OF THE BIG GUY IN ACTION ON TONIGHT'S "METROPOLIS EDITION."

AND I GOT SOME GREAT SHOTS OF HIM PUTTING OUT THAT FIRE LAST NIGHT IN SUICIDE SLUM!

I COULD LET YOU HAVE THEM IN EXCHANGE FOR, *OH, I dunno*, A *JOB* ON THE PHOTO STAFF?

YOU NEVER QUIT, DO YOU, OLSEN?

I'LL GIVE YOU FIFTY BUCKS.

SOLD!

AND WHAT ABOUT *YOU*, KENT? I KNOW YOU'RE THE NEW GUY ON THE CITY DESK...

...BUT WHAT ARE YOUR THOUGHTS ON OUR STRANGE VISITOR FROM ANOTHER PLANET?

SORRY, PERRY. I'M AFRAID I HAVEN'T HAD ENOUGH CONTACT WITH SUPERMAN TO FORM AN OPINION.

WELL, LET'S STAY ON THIS, PEOPLE.

OUR READERS WANT INFORMATION ON SUPERMAN AND THEY WANT IT *NOW!*

Y'KNOW, THESE PHOTOS REALLY AREN'T BAD.

THANKS, CHIEF!

DON'T CALL ME CHIEF!

INFORMATION! THAT WILL BE OUR MOST POTENT WEAPON IN THE BATTLE AGAINST THIS THREAT, THIS... "SUPERMAN!"

HOW FORTUNATE MY PEOPLE WERE ABLE TO SALVAGE THE MEMORY UNIT FROM THE LEXO-SKEL'S COMPUTERIZED BRAIN.

NOW I CAN STUDY SUPERMAN IN ACTION AND PLAN MY ATTACK AROUND HIS LIMITATIONS.

BUT WHY ATTACK *AT ALL,* LEX? DO YOU THINK HE'S DANGEROUS?

SUPERMAN IS AN UNKNOWN ENTITY, MERCY. I *DISTRUST* THE UNKNOWN.

9

THE LATEST ADVANCE IN LEXCORP TECHNOLOGY IS READY FOR A TRIAL RUN ON THE KAZNIAN EMBASSY.

WHY THERE?

HAVE YOU FORGOTTEN THE REGENT OF KAZNIA STILL REFUSES TO PAY THE BILLION DOLLARS FOR MY *LEXO-SKEL 5000*?

EVEN THOUGH CORBE... FAILED TO DELIVE... IT, I INSIST O... COMPENSATION

SO YOU'RE SENDING YOUR OWN "SUPERMAN" TO SETTLE THE ACCOUNT.

"EXACTLY."

SUPERMAN SPEAKS!
Exclusive Interview by Lois Lane

FLYING MAN SAVES JET

SUPERMAN F... TERRORIST...

LOOKS LIKE YOU'VE MADE QUITE A NAME FOR YOURSELF, SON.

COME ON, TURPIN! LET ME THROUGH!

I SAID NO REPORTERS, LANE! THAT GOES DOUBLE FOR YOU!

LOIS CAN HANDLE THE POLICE WITH HER USUAL TACT AND DIPLOMACY.

FORTUNATELY...

I'LL MAKE SURE YOU GET A SPECIAL MENTION IN MY ARTICLE, DAN! HOW DO YOU SPELL "THICKHEAD"?

DON'T PLAY TOUGH WITH ME, MISSY!

...I HAVE ANOTHER OPTION.

WHATEVER DID THIS WAS BIG, POWERFUL, AND UNLESS I MISS MY GUESS...

...STILL IN THE AREA!

18

PINK!

SPANK!

STILL BREATHING, ALIEN? YOUR STAMINA IS NOTHING IF NOT IMPRESSIVE.

WHOOM!

HERE'S ANOTHER TRICK YOU'LL LIKE!

SSZT!

OH, YES. YOUR HEAT VISION.

AS YOU SEE, I'VE ACCOUNTED FOR THAT, TOO.

ZAAAKr

ARRGH!

AND WHILE YOU MAY BE POWER-FUL, I'M REASONABLY SURE YOU CAN'T SURVIVE UNDER WATER.

THIS IS HOW IT ENDS THEN, SUPERMAN. YOU ARE DISPATCHED AS QUICKLY AS YOU ARRIVED.

A CURIOSITY, A FREAK, THAT CAUGHT THE PUBLIC'S EYE FOR A MOMENT, THEN VANISHED, LEAVING ONLY AN UNPLEASANT MEMORY.

FAREWELL.

23

I THINK NOW WOULD BE A GOOD TIME TO MAKE GENERAL HARDCASTLE AN OFFER ON MY LATEST LINE OF DEFENSE ANDROIDS.

YOU NEVER KNOW WHEN A HOSTILE ALIEN MIGHT TURN UP.

LUTHOR, HERE, GENERAL. THE SUPERMAN THREAT HAS BEEN *NEU-TRALIZED.*

UH, LEX? *LEX!*

HE'S *FREE!*

NO! IT'S NOT *POSSIBLE!*

LUTHOR? LUTHOR? ARE YOU *THERE?*

CREATORS

PAUL DINI WRITER

Writer Paul Dini has earned five Emmy Awards for his work on *Batman: The Animated Series*, *Superman: The Animated Series*, and *Justice League Unlimited*. His live-action work includes story editing for *Lost*. In comics, his *Batman Adventures: Mad Love*, with artist Bruce Timm, won numerous awards. In 2006, he was head writer for DC's *Countdown to Infinite Crisis* and took over Batman's adventures in *Detective Comics*. More recently, he wrote the Batman-based series *Gotham City Sirens* and *Batman: Streets of Gotham*.

RICK BURCHETT PENCILLER

Rick Burchett has worked as a comics artist for more than 25 years. He has received the comics industry's Eisner Award three times, Spain's Haxtur Award, and he has been nominated for the Eagle Award. Rick lives with his wife and two sons in Missouri, USA.

TERRY AUSTIN INKER

Throughout his career, inker Terry Austin has received dozens of awards for his work on high-profile comics for DC Comics and Marvel, such as *The Uncanny X-Men*, *Doctor Strange*, *Justice League America*, *Green Lantern*, and *Superman Adventures*. He lives in New York, USA.

GLOSSARY

blatant obvious and shameless

cynic person who believes that selfishness is the primary motivation for people

degenerate to become worse or inferior in quality, or a person who is immoral or a criminal

dissent disagreement with an idea or opinion

duplicate copy, or double

exclusive story that appears in one place only

extermination killing of large amounts of people or animals

fortunate lucky

hostile unfriendly or angry

inflicts causes suffering to someone or something

potent powerful or strong

retaliation act of revenge

salvage to rescue property from a shipwreck, fire, or other disaster

simulate pretend or fake

SUPERMAN GLOSSARY

Clark Kent: Superman's alter ego, Clark Kent, is a reporter for the *Daily Planet* newspaper and was raised by Ma and Pa Kent. No one knows he is Superman except for his adopted parents, the Kents.

The Daily Planet: the city of Metropolis's biggest and most read newspaper. Clark, Lois, Jimmy, and Perry all work for the *Daily Planet*.

Invulnerability: Superman's invulnerability makes him impervious to harm. Almost nothing can hurt him -- except for Kryptonite, a radioactive rock from his home planet, Krypton.

Jimmy Olsen: Jimmy is a cub reporter and photographer. He is also a friend to Lois and Clark.

The Kent Family: Ma and Pa Kent found Superman when he crashed to Earth from his home planet, Krypton. They raised him as their own child, giving him the name Clark.

Lex Luthor: Lex believes Superman is a threat to Earth and must be stopped. He will do anything it takes to bring the Man of Steel to his knees.

Lois Lane: like Clark Kent, Lois is a reporter at the *Daily Planet*. She is also one of Clark's best friends.

Metropolis: the city where Clark Kent (Superman) lives.

Perry White: Clark's boss at the *Daily Planet* newspaper. He has a temper and can be very impatient sometimes.

1. In this panel, Clark Kent pretends to not know Superman. Why do you think it's important for him to keep his other identity a secret? Explain your answer.

...BUT WHAT ARE YOUR THOUGHTS ON OUR STRANGE VISITOR FROM ANOTHER PLANET?

SORRY, PERRY I'M AFRAID I HAVEN'T HAD ENOUGH CONTACT WITH SUPERMAN TO FORM AN OPINION.

WELL, 'S STAY N THIS, EOPLE.

OUR READERS WANT INFORMATION ON SUPERMAN AND THEY WANT IT NOW!

Y'KNOW, THESE PHOTOS REALLY AREN'T

2. The woman in the black outfit is Mercy Graves, an employee of Lex Luthor's. Based on the panel below, what role do you think she plays in his company? Explain.

GET DOWN!

KRAMM!

GET DOWN!

3. What do you think Lex's motivations are for getting rid of Superman? Is he concerned for Metropolis? Does he want to get rid of his competition? Explain your answer by referencing specific panels in this book.

4. Of all Superman's skills, which ones turned out to be the most helpful in this book? If you could have any of Superman's superpowers, which one would you want? Why would you choose that power?

SUPERMAN ADVENTURES

Raintree